Mike **FABAREZ**

EXPLORING *the*
GOSPEL

Being *sure* you're right with God

EXPLORING THE GOSPEL

Being Sure You're Right with God
© Mike Fabarez 2014

Except where otherwise indicated, all Scripture quotations in this manual are taken from the English Standard Version (ESV), Wheaton, IL: Crossway Bibles, a publishing ministry of Good News Publishers, 2007.

For publication or distribution information contact:
Dr. Mike Fabarez
Focal Point Radio Ministries
P.O. Box 2850
Laguna Hills, California 92654
Toll Free: (888) 320-5885
Voice: (949) 389-0476
Fax: (949) 389-0475
Email: info@fpr.info
Web: www.focalpointradio.org

INTRODUCTION

It is hard to argue with the wisdom of the old carpenter's advice: "Measure twice, cut once!" And how often in the middle of one of those do-it-yourself projects have I wished that I had heeded that advice. But I guess when you're talking about a wooden two-by-four or a piece of plywood, you can always spend the extra time and money to get another one and try it again.

Unfortunately, when it comes to our lives, there are no "do overs." We get one shot at it. To put it in the words of the Bible: "It is appointed for man to die once, and after that comes judgment" (Hebrews 9:27). "You only go around once in this life," as they say, and so we had better be sure that when it is over we are ready to meet our Maker.

That's where "measuring twice" comes in. I have met many people who think they are "right with God" because they wrongly assume that they've done what the Bible says they must do to be "ready." Many draw that conclusion based on their recollection of a few Bible verses they've heard from a preacher or read in a religious pamphlet. Some have even read the New Testament for themselves and believe they have the basic idea. But when we consider something as important as our lives and our eternal destiny, we had better take time to revisit what the Bible says and be absolutely certain.

Exploring the Gospel is all about carefully digging into the Bible's information for ourselves. It is about rethinking and reexamining the message of how we can be sure that our lives are right with our Creator. It is a step-by-step guide that will lead us to interact with several passages from the Bible, which present how we must all respond to the life and work of Jesus Christ.

I invite you to dig into the following pages with a heart and mind that are ready to honestly reconsider what the Bible says and does not say about life, death, heaven, and hell. So grab a Bible and look up every text that is listed and discussed. And every time you read a question and see a blank space, take a pen and thoughtfully write out your response.

Your life and eternal destiny are much too important to casually assume or hope that you have the message of the gospel all figured out. So, explore it carefully all over again from the beginning, and be sure you are right with God.

Therefore, if anyone is in Christ, he is a new creation. The old has passed away; behold, the new has come.

2 Corinthians 5:17

THE BIG CONCERN

The concern over being "right with God" is as old as the third chapter of the Bible. Ever since Adam and Eve's first rebellious act in the Garden of Eden men and women have been faced with the problem of a severed relationship with their Creator. People with sin on their record can't create nor maintain a relationship with a holy and sinless God. For centuries people have tried, and they still do, but by themselves imperfect people just don't have a chance.

The good news is that Jesus came to solve the problem (that's even what the word "gospel" actually means)! What he did made all the difference in the world for people wanting to be right with their Maker. Unfortunately, too many people don't understand what the good news is all about. They struggle through life hoping that their good deeds will outweigh their bad deeds—as though God will simply overlook their sin and embrace a 65% righteous person.

Being "right with God" is certainly not defined by doing more good than bad. Jesus made that clear in his promise to a dying thief[1]. Doing good things may be an important part of living the Christian life, but if one wants to be "right with God" it all comes down to a question of one's relationship to Jesus Christ. Heaven and hell will ultimately be about who really "knows" Jesus and who does not.

MOST PEOPLE

Though there are always some who admit to being on God's bad list, most people believe that they are "right with God." They may be counting on a divine sliding scale, or some religious ritual, but whatever their reason, most people think that come judgment day they'll probably come out on top. Unfortunately, that is not what the Bible says. Read *Matthew 7:13-14*. What does this passage have to say about how many really do inherit God's blessing after their death?

---

[1] See Luke 23:39-43 if you are unfamiliar with this story.

THINK
About It

Based on the deception that is depicted in Matthew 7. Do you believe that you are, or ever have been, deceived about the reality of your "right standing" before God?

Read a few verses further in *Matthew 7:22-23* where those standing before Jesus present their case. Though they seem certain about their right standing before God, Jesus tells them to depart from him because in reality "he never knew them" and they still had sin on their record. What is your reaction to Jesus' prediction of there being so many deceived people on judgment day?

With so much deception and so much on the line, it is critically important that we look to the Bible to discover just exactly *what a Christian is, how a person becomes a Christian, and how we will know when we are a Christian.*

WHAT IS A CHRISTIAN?

The word "Christian" is not often used in the Bible (actually only three times[2]) and yet it was the label that caught on to refer to someone who is closely aligned with Jesus Christ. It may mean different things to different people today, but when the term was coined a person who was closely aligned with Jesus was someone who truly "knew" him and was "known by him" (remember the words of Jesus in Matthew 7:23).

This is obviously more than just knowing *about* Jesus. Really knowing Jesus implies a relationship with him—a good relationship. Notice how Jesus described it.

> *"I am the good shepherd; I know my own and my own know me, just as the Father knows me and I know the Father"*
>
> *John 10:14-15a*

---

2 Acts 11:26; 26:28; 1 Peter 4:16.

Jesus compares his relationship with his people to his relationship with God the Father. It is clear then that to "know Jesus" is to have a real and vital relationship with Jesus. But it doesn't stop there.

> *Jesus answered, "You know neither me nor my Father. If you knew me, you would know my Father also."*
>
> *John 8:19b*

If we have a vital relationship with Jesus Christ, we also have a real and vital relationship with God the Father. The sin problem that severed our relationship with our Creator has been solved for those who "know Christ."

A CHRISTIAN IS SOMEONE WHO IS ACCEPTABLE TO GOD

Christians then, are those people who through Christ have had their sins forgiven and have been made acceptable before a perfect and sinless God. Christians are imperfect people made perfect in God's sight through their alignment with Jesus Christ!

> *"Let it be known to you therefore, brothers, that through this man forgiveness of sins is proclaimed to you,"*
>
> *Acts 13:38*

> *There is therefore now no condemnation for those who are in Christ Jesus.*
>
> *Romans 8:1*

How does it make you feel to know that as a Christian you can be completely, 100% acceptable before God?

A CHRISTIAN IS SOMEONE WHO FOLLOWS CHRIST

One of the most popular words in the New Testament for one aligned with Jesus Christ is the word "disciple." The word "disciple" is a descriptive term for one who follows the teachings of his master and seeks to emulate the lifestyle of his master. In the Bible those who had been made right with God through their faith in Christ sought to follow Christ. Though a Christian's following of Christ and his teachings is never consistently perfect, the New Testament speaks volumes about this being a clear indication of those who know Christ and those who don't.

Read *1 John 3:1-10* and summarize what is being said in that passage.

A CHRISTIAN IS SOMEONE WHO HAS BEEN ADOPTED BY GOD

First John 3:1 reminds us of another popular biblical phrase used to described Christians, namely the "children of God." This title emphasizes the strong legal bond that exists between God and his people. With their sins forgiven and their lives made acceptable to him through the work of Christ, Christians are brought into a close and permanent relationship with God as his adopted children. The indwelling of the Holy Spirit is described in Ephesians 1:5, 13-14 as the pledge of God's adoption.

Ponder the power of this concept for a moment. God, our infinitely wise Creator, has chosen to embrace Christians not just as subjects in his kingdom but as sons and daughters in his family!

> *...but you have received the Spirit of adoption as sons, by whom we cry, "Abba! [3] Father!"*
>
> *Romans 8:15b*

---

[3] "Abba" is an Aramaic term of endearment for one's father.

A CHRISTIAN IS SOMEONE WHO IS CLOSELY IDENTIFIED WITH OTHER CHRISTIANS

The most frequently used term in the New Testament for those aligned with Christ is "brothers." This may come as a surprise considering that it speaks of our relationship with each other instead of our relationship with God. Jesus obviously wanted us to realize that Christianity was not to be as "personal" as our generation has wanted to make it.

Christians are called to find an identity together. Assembled groups of Christians are called the body of Christ, a temple of God, a household of faith, and a flock of followers, just to name a few. The love, unity, togetherness, and mutual respect of Christians for one another should be one of our distinguishing marks.

> *"By this all people will know that you are my disciples, if you have love for one another."*
>
> *John 13:35*

This brief overview of what a Christian is should quickly reveal that one cannot be "sort of a Christian." There must be a point in one's life when one becomes a Christian. Though one can consider Christianity and learn tons about it from the inside of a church (possibly for years), a person is either a Christian or not a Christian. There is no middle ground.

THINK
About It

What are some of the popular misconceptions concerning what a Christian is?

HOW DO I BECOME A CHRISTIAN?

To be sure about our relationship with God we must be certain that we are clear about what the Bible says a person must do to become a Christian.

TO BECOME A CHRISTIAN YOU MUST UNDERSTAND THE GOSPEL

The New Testament boldly proclaims a message (called "the gospel") that if rightly understood and rightly responded to makes one a Christian. This is what most of the preaching recorded in the book of Acts is all about. In some of the gospel presentations in the New Testament we will find much time allotted to laying a foundation and giving background, in other instances we will simply find a record of the speaker calling the people to rightly respond to an abbreviated gospel message. In any case, a pattern emerges that gives us a basic outline of the gospel content.

Summary of the
GOSPEL MESSAGE

1. The Background
- *God is our Creator*
- *God is Holy*
- *God is Just*
- *God is Loving*

2. The Bad News
- *We are Sinful and Separated from God*
- *We Deserve God's Punishment*

3. The Good News
- *Jesus is God*
- *He Lived and Died as Our Substitute*
- *He Conquered Death for Us*

THINK
About It

Look at Acts 17:22-34 as one example of the gospel message being presented to non-Christians. Attempt to locate as many of the elements in the above summary outline as possible.

Remember that this is just the gospel message. It does not spell out the necessary and biblical response (to be discussed later beginning on page 15). Nevertheless, one cannot become a Christian without understanding and embracing the basic message of the gospel. So it is important to look at each element a little closer.

GOD IS OUR CREATOR.

The background to the gospel message is rooted in the fact that we are created by God. This is so important that we find it in the very first verse of the Bible. Why do you think that this is so essential if one is to properly understand the rest of the gospel message? What are the implications for people if God really is their Creator?

GOD IS HOLY.

This means that God is absolutely perfect. Read *1 Peter 1:15-16* and notice that God's own perfection is to be the standard for all those he has created. This concept of perfection being the only acceptable standard is central in the gospel message!

GOD IS JUST.

God has not left the people he made to do whatever they want without accountability and consequences for their choices. Foundational to the gospel message is the fact that God will one day judge each person, and according to the Bible he will do it with perfect justice. Job 34:12 says, "*God will not do wickedly and the Almighty will not pervert justice.*" That may sound like a comforting verse if someone has seriously wronged us, but assuming that we by nature have all seriously wronged God (failing to measure up to his standards of perfection) the justice of God leaves us in a precarious position. What does *2 Thessalonians 1:8-9* say about the end result of God's justice for most people?

GOD IS LOVE.

Understanding that we all answer to our Creator, that he requires perfect holiness, and that because he is just he can't bend the rules, should make it overwhelmingly clear that if there is going to be any "good news" it will have to stem from his love! Thankfully, God *is* loving (1 John 4:8). His love prompted him to provide a solution for our problem of sin and the coming judgment. A person cannot become a Christian unless he first understands something about that problem. We've called this "the bad news." The gospel is good news because it provides answers for people's terrible dilemma.

WE ARE SINFUL AND SEPARATED.

Many people are slow to admit that they have this problem because they have come to believe that sin is doing something they consider "really bad" or culturally unacceptable. Remember that God, by virtue of his position as our Creator, is the judge of whether something is bad or good. Some things our culture may consider moral may in fact be immoral to God (Luke 16:15). In the Bible sin is defined in two ways. First, it describes doing something God considers wrong (1 John 3:4 – i.e. breaking his standard). Secondly, it describes the state of being separated from God (Ephesians 2:1 – i.e. living without a relationship with God). Realize that people who do not have a relationship with God are considered to be in a state of sin even though they may do many things that are morally acceptable.

How does *Isaiah 59:2* summarize what happened in the garden of Eden when Adam and Eve sinned?

By reading Isaiah 59:2 and noting that sin causes separation, we might be led to believe that we become separated from God (enter the state of sin) when we commit our first sinful act. But in reality the Bible teaches that every person since Adam has been born into a state of sin. Comment on the relationship between the state of sin and the acts of sin in *Ephesians 4:18-19*.

WE DESERVE GOD'S PUNISHMENT.

Many people believe that "guilt" is simply a bad feeling we have when we do bad things. In reality, the Bible defines guilt as being responsible for sin. We do not necessarily have to feel guilty to be guilty. According to the Bible all people who live in a state of sin and choose to do sinful things are guilty before a just and holy God. That means that all people are deserving of God's punishment.

When someone becomes convinced of the bad news regarding their situation before God they are ready to hear the greatest news of the gospel message. The great news is all about Jesus Christ!

JESUS IS GOD.

This is an essential part of the gospel message in the New Testament (notice that it becomes a test of one's Christian profession in 1 John 4:2-3). Jesus was the expected Messiah that had been foretold in the Old Testament which, if carefully examined, clearly pointed to someone who was more than a mere human (see for instance Micah 5:2; Isaiah 9:6; Daniel 7:13-14). Jesus had to be God for his work on our behalf to be qualitatively and quantitatively adequate to save us. It was "qualitatively divine" in that he lived

THINK
About It

Ponder the importance of Jesus being God, and any experiences you might have had with those who try to convince people that Jesus is not God.

a perfectly holy life (1 John 3:5; 1 Peter 2:22), and "quantitatively divine" in that his death was applicable for many (Hebrews 7:27; 9:14). Read Philippians 2:6-8 and comment on what Jesus went through in becoming a man to accomplish our salvation.

JESUS LIVED AND DIED AS OUR SUBSTITUTE.

This is the core of the gospel message. When we thought through God's holiness it became clear that a 65% righteous life would not cut it with a perfect God. He, by the nature of his holiness, requires 100% righteousness and 0% sin. Knowing that all humans are sinful and separated from him, God the Father sent Jesus to become a man and live a 100% perfect life. This perfect righteousness can then be credited to people who are not perfectly righteous.

Not only did Jesus live so that he could give us his righteousness, he died so that he could take on our sins. When Jesus died on the cross, God the Father was exercising his justice against the sinful acts of sinful people by punishing Jesus instead of them. In this way God could credit Christ's account with our sin and leave us with none! Notice carefully how this is stated in the Bible:

> *For our sake he made him to be sin who knew no sin, so that in him we might become the righteousness of God.*
> *2 Corinthians 5:21*

Our Creator demonstrates his incredible love for us by counting Jesus' life and death as a substitution for ours, making us in Christ 100% righteous and 0% sinful, while at the same time maintaining his holiness and justice. This is the heart of the gospel message!

JESUS CONQUERED DEATH FOR US.

The result of all of this is that God is now able to free us from the penalty of our sin, which includes both spiritual death (i.e., relational separation from God) and physical death (i.e., our spirit's separation from our bodies). In taking care of the sin problem Jesus has eliminated for Christians the relational separation that existed between him and us. The intimate relationship with God that Christians enjoy every day is proof that Christ's life and death did the job and bridged the gap!

Jesus also demonstrated that he had fully paid the price for our sins in that he reversed the biological consequence of sin—physical death. This is what his resurrection was all about! While one might claim that the "proof" of a real and intimate relationship with an invisible God is hardly proof, it is difficult to argue with Christ's resurrection! This is God's objective, historical stamp of approval on the substitutionary life and death of Jesus Christ. Read *1 Corinthians 15:12-28* and comment on how important Jesus' resurrection is in the Bible.

THINK
About It

If you ever have doubts about the truthfulness of the gospel message a thorough investigation of the resurrection of Jesus should be a top priority. Researching this objective proof of the gospel has won over many skeptics!

TO BECOME A CHRISTIAN YOU MUST RIGHTLY RESPOND TO THE GOSPEL.

Knowing and accepting the facts of the gospel message are critcally important, but it is not enough. God requires that if a person is to become a Christian he or she must respond to the gospel message as directed in the Bible. God calls people to *make a decision* based on the gospel facts. This decision involves two parts. Note the two components of this decision as stated in Acts 20:21.

> *"testifying both to Jews and to Greeks of repentance toward God and of faith in our Lord Jesus Christ."*
>
> *Acts 20:21*

Let's look at each part one at a time.

TURN TO GOD IN REPENTANCE.

Repentance is presented over and over again in the New Testament as a necessary response to the gospel. Carefully read this partial list of examples below.

> *From that time Jesus began to preach, saying, "Repent, for the kingdom of heaven is at hand."*
>
> *Matthew 4:17*

> *Jesus came into Galilee, proclaiming the gospel of God, and saying, "The time is fulfilled, and the kingdom of God is at hand; repent and believe in the gospel."*
>
> *Mark 1: 14b-15*

> *...but unless you repent, you will all likewise perish.*
>
> *Luke 13:3b*

> *for I have five brothers. -so that he may warn them, lest they also come into this place of torment.' But Abraham said, 'They have Moses and the Prophets; let them hear them.' And he said, 'No, father Abraham, but if someone goes to them from the dead, they will repent.'*
>
> *Luke 16:28-30*

and said to them, "Thus it is written, that the Christ should suffer and on the third day rise from the dead, and that repentance and forgiveness of sins should be proclaimed in his name to all nations, beginning from Jerusalem.
Luke 24:46-47

Repent, therefore, and turn again, that your sins may be blotted out
Acts 3:19

And they glorified God, saying, "Then to the Gentiles also God has granted repentance that leads to life."
Acts 11:18b

The times of ignorance God overlooked, but now he commands all people everywhere to repent, because he has fixed a day on which he will judge the world in righteousness by a man whom he has ap pointed; and of this he has given assurance to all by raising him from the dead.
Acts 17:30-31

For godly grief produces a repentance that leads to salvation with out regret, whereas worldly grief produces death.
2 Corinthians 7:10a

Therefore let us leave the elementary doctrine of Christ and go on to maturity, not laying again a foundation of repentance from dead works, and of faith toward God,
Hebrews 6:1

The Lord is not slow to fulfill his promise, as some count slowness, but is is patient toward you, not wishing that any should perish, but that all should reach repentance.
2 Peter 3:9

It is easy to see from this list that repentance is of primary importance! To properly respond to the gospel and become a Christian one must repent! In its most literal sense the word "repent" is a command that tells people that they should "completely change their thinking" which inevitably changes their behavior. Or as one lexicographer puts it, to repent is *"to change one's way of life as the result of a complete change of thought and attitude with regard to sin and righteousness."*[4]

This Greek word that we translate "repent" in the Bible is the same word that the ancient Hellenistic army commanders used to get their marching soldiers to turn around 180°. When they wanted their men to do an "about-face" they shouted, "Repent!"

To repent is to make a mental decision to turn around. It is critically important that we know what the gospel is telling us to turn from, and what the gospel is telling us to turn to. Use the following passages to answer those two questions: *1 Thessalonians 1:8-9; Acts 20:21;* and *Acts 14:15.*

THINK
About It

What it is like to make a decision to become a Christian that involves this kind of mental 180°?

---

4 Johannes P. Louw and Eugene A. Nida, Greek-English Lexicon of the New Testament based on Semantic Domains, (New York: United Bible Societies) 1988, 1989.

HAVE FAITH IN OUR LORD JESUS.

The second component of God's required response to the gospel is to place one's faith in the Lord Jesus Christ. If one has truly understood the gospel message it is not hard to see the absolute necessity of discarding any trust in one's personal righteousness (which is totally deficient before a perfect God) and having all one's trust in Jesus' righteousness (which is 100% complete). Notice this fundamental definition of saving faith as the Apostle Paul describes his new attitude toward all his "accomplishments" in trying to be righteous and acceptable to God without Christ.

> *For his sake I have suffered the loss of all things and count them as rubbish, in order that I may gain Christ and be found in him, not having a righteousness of my own that comes from the law, but that which comes through faith in Christ, the righteousness from God that depends on faith.*
>
> *Philippians 3:8b-9*

To put my faith in Christ means that I cease trusting in my own résumé and from that point on I keep my confidence in Jesus Christ alone as the sole provision for my sinful condition!

Notice that the words used to describe faith are words like "trust" and "confidence." This is important. Unfortunately, misunderstandings about "faith" abound because over time our English word "faith" has lost its impact and is often understood as merely "believing" the truthfulness of some facts (unfortunately, sometimes even the original Greek word is translated this way in our Bibles). Though our English dictionaries still offer a secondary definition of "belief" as having "firm faith, confidence, or trust: I believe in your ability to solve the problem"[5] most understand "belief" as simply agreeing, or giving mental assent to some proposed facts.

This has led to the false impression that to be a Christian one has to simply agree with the facts presented in the gospel message. This is a terribly costly misconception. The Bible

---

[5] American Heritage Dictionary: Third Edition, Softkey International Inc., 1994.

points this out by reminding us that even the demons have a proper set of beliefs in the facts (James 2:19). "Faith" is not just believing the facts, instead real faith means transferring our trust and confidence to Jesus Christ. If a person is to become a Christian he or she must be trusting in Jesus' perfect life and his substitutionary death that he suffered in order to pay the just penalty for sin.

As you read the numerous examples of the gospel's call to "faith" you will discover that the necessary response to trust in Christ is not just for the future day of judgment, but its emphasis is very much on the here-and-now! The gospel is calling us to trust in Jesus not only to save us in the future, but also to lead us in the present. Jesus demonstrated this aspect of faith while he was here on earth by continually calling people to "follow him." After Jesus' departure the Apostles often spoke of trusting "the Lord" Jesus. The emphasis here is on his position as leader or boss of one's life. Though he is not on earth presently to physically follow and emulate, he laid down a clear pattern of living that is to be followed with the help and guidance of God's Spirit.

> *Whoever says he abides in him ought to walk in the same way in which he walked.*
>
> *1 John 2:6*

When we place our trust in Christ it is a confidence for a future deliverance from judgment *as well* as a confidence in the present lordship of Christ for our daily lives.

HOW DO I KNOW THAT I REALLY AM A CHRISTIAN?

Of course the most obvious way that we can know that we are Christians is to be certain that we have properly understood the gospel and have rightly responded to it. Assuming that a person is convinced of this we will briefly examine the objective indicators that give assurance of one's salvation.

REAL CHRISTIANS BEAR REAL FRUIT

Wanting to avoid the tragic self-deception of would-be Christians, who discover on judgment day that they were never really Christians after all (Matthew 7:22-23). Let us seek to compare our lives with the primary test of true Christianity-namely, a transformed life!

When we become Christians our lives are changed forever in a variety of profound ways. Some patterns in our lives cease and others begin.

Therefore, if anyone is in Christ, he is a new creation. The old has passed away: behold, the new has come.
2 Corinthians 5:17

The Bible often calls these obvious changes caused by our new relationship with Christ "fruit." Fruit is an appropriate analogy for these changes in our lives because, like fruit that is borne on a tree, these new patterns of behavior are produced as the result of God's Spirit working in and through us.

"By this my Father is glorified, that you bear much fruit and so prove to be my disciples."
John 15:8

These changes are so profound that Jesus once equated the beginning of this new relationship with him to being "born again" (John 3:3). These changes include the transformation of one's core motivation, the curbing of one's sinful habits, and the initiation of new righteous habits – all of which are promised to last for a lifetime! Let's examine each of these.

THINK *About It*

What overall changes have you and others witnessed in your life since you became a Christian?

REAL CHRISTIANITY TRANSFORMS YOUR CORE MOTIVATIONS.

The Bible is clear that everyone is born sinful. We all come into this world separated from God and wired to please ourselves. We may choose to do this in culturally acceptable ways, but we are still motivated by a desire to live for "self."

When we become Christians this motivation is turned upside-down!

> *"he died for all, that those who live might no longer live for themselves but for him who for their sake died and was raised."*
>
> *2 Corinthians 5:15*

In what ways do you see that your core motivations are different than before?

REAL CHRISTIANITY CURBS YOUR SINFUL HABITS.

Christians still sin (1 John 1:10 – 2:1), but not at all like they used to! Sinful habits and continuous indulgence in sinful behaviors are broken when God gets involved in a person's life. Where you once found addictions and vices in a non-Christian's life, you now find freedom and deliverance in the Christian's life (see 1 Corinthians 6:9-11). If there is a continuing pattern of habitual disobedience in people's lives, even though they may claim to be Christians, they are deceived about the genuineness of their relationship with Christ.

> *And by this we know that we have come to know him, if we keep his commandments. Whoever says, "I know him," but does not keep his commandments is a liar, and the truth is not in him.*
>
> *1 John 2:3-4*

The curbing of sinful behavior is inevitable because Jesus came not only to remove sin from our record, but he also came to remove sin from our lives!

You know that he appeared to take away sins, and in him there is no sin. No one who abides in him keeps on sinning; no one who keeps on sinning has either seen him or known him. Little children, let no one deceive you. Whoever practices righteousness is righteous, as he is righteous. Whoever makes a practice of sinning is of the devil, for the devil has been sinning from the beginning. The reason the Son of God appeared was to destroy the works of the devil. No one born of God makes a practice of sinning, for God's seed abides in him, and he cannot keep on sinning because he has been born of God. By this it is evident who are the children of God, and who are the children of the devil: whoever does not practice righteousness is not of God, nor is the one who does not love his brother.

1 John 3:5-10

In what ways have your sinful habits been curbed?

REAL CHRISTIANITY INITIATES NEW RIGHTEOUS HABITS.

If we have truly repented of our sins and placed our trust in Christ, righteous habits naturally follow. Notice what the Bible says about the "proof" of real repentance and real faith.

...they should repent and turn to God, performing deeds in keeping with their repentance."

Acts 26:20b

What good is it, my brothers, if someone says he has faith but does not have works? Can that faith save him? ... So also faith by itself, if it does not have works, is dead. But someone will say, "You have faith; and I have works." Show me your faith apart from your works, and I will show you my faith by my works.

James 2:14, 17-18

A sure indicator that we have truly turned to God is the presence of good and righteous deeds. These new patterns of doing what God desires for us to do are not drudgery! Because of the transformation of our core motivation doing what is right is a joy for the genuine Christian.

By this we know that we love the children of God, when we love God and obey his commandments. For this is the love of God, that we keep his commandments. And his commandments are not burdensome.

1 John 5:2-3

What righteous habits has God initiated in your life?

REAL CHRISTIANITY CREATES CHANGES THAT LAST A LIFETIME.

When God genuinely transforms people, the effects of that transformation last for the rest of their lives. Of course there will be times of struggle and occasional defeat but their new life in Christ is never temporary. Notice the Bible's perspective when people's association with Christ *is* temporary.

They went out from us, but they were not of us; for if they had been of us, they would have continued with us. But they went out, that it might become plain that they all are not of us.

1 John 2:19

For those adopted into God's family (or flock in this case) there is nothing that can sever that new relationship. It is an act of God that cannot be reversed.

"My sheep hear my voice, and I know them, and they follow me. I give them eternal life, and they will never perish, and no one will snatch them out of my hand. My Father, who has given them to me, is greater than all, and no one is able to snatch them out of the Father's hand."

John 10:27-29

If the Christian's relationship with Jesus is secure, then it follows that the implications and effects of this relationship with Christ are equally secure.

How does this principle of guaranteed longevity in Christ help to convert verses like the one below from passages producing fear and concern into passages that produce security and confidence?

"For we have come to share in Christ, if indeed we hold our original confidence firm to the end."

Hebrews 3:14

BIG ERRORS REGARDING CHRISTIANITY & GOOD DEEDS!

So far we have studied 1) the right gospel, 2) the proper response to the gospel, and 3) the good deeds that follow. It is critical that we understand the relationship between these elements and never confuse them. Confusing the role of any of the elements we have discussed can have disastrous results. There are two primary ways that people tend to misunderstand them.

The first error is a fatal one. Almost every cult group in the world falls into this trap. Notice that though they may include the proper elements they certainly don't understand them as presented in the Bible because they place them wrongly into the biblical equation. The first popular error looks like this:

Those who believe this equation say that if you want to become a Christian you must:

1) understand the gospel;
2) respond to the gospel with repentance and faith;
3) do a lot of good deeds;

...and then you will become a Christian!

When we took a closer look at faith earlier in this chapter it became clear that the call to faith was a call to put our trust in Christ, and Christ alone. We saw that we must abandon any confidence in our own righteousness and trust fully in the righteousness that comes from Jesus Christ. The equation above bases our salvation (at least in part) on the accomplishment of our own good deeds. This is thoroughly unbiblical! Notice in the following verses that our good deeds play no role in bringing about our salvation. We are saved through the work of Christ and what he has done for us, not what we have accomplished ourselves!

"But when the goodness and loving kindness of God our Savior appeared, he saved us, not because of works done by us in righteousness, but according to his own mercy,"

Titus 3:4-5a

"For by grace you have been saved through faith. And this is not your own doing; it is the gift of God, not a result of works, so that no one may boast."

Ephesians 2:8-9

THINK
About It

What groups are you familiar with who say that good works are the basis for our salvation (wholly or in part)?

These verses make it clear that our salvation is not based on the good deeds that we do. Unfortunately, some have understood these verses to mean that good works are not important in the equation at all. That is the second big error people can make when thinking through the elements involved in salvation.

When people take good deeds and fruit out of the equation altogether it looks something like this:

1	2	3
the **GOSPEL**	*the* **RESPONSE**	*being a* **CHRISTIAN**
+	**=**	

They would say, if you want to be sure you are a Christian just make sure that:

1) you have understood the gospel;
2) you have responded to the gospel;

...then you can be sure you are a Christian regardless of whether you see any fruit of that decision or not.

We have already seen that this is an unacceptable equation according to the Bible. Real Christians produce real fruit! Jesus said:

"You will recognize them by their fruits. Are grapes gathered from thornbushes, or figs from thistles? So, every healthy tree bears good fruit, but the diseased tree bears bad fruit. A healthy tree cannot bear bad fruit, nor can a diseased tree bear good fruit. Every tree that does not bear good fruit is cut down and thrown into the fire. Thus you will recognize them by their fruits."

Matthew 7:16-20

SUMMARY!

The gospel message properly understood, coupled with a biblical response to the gospel (repentance & faith) makes one a Christian who then bears fruit (good deeds). An accurate summary of the gospel elements should look like this:

1 *the* **GOSPEL** + 2 *the* **RESPONSE** = *being a* **CHRISTIAN** + 3 *good* **DEEDS**

If you want to be sure that you are a Christian you should evaluate your life and make sure that:

1) you have understood the gospel as presented in the Bible;
2) you have rightly responded to the gospel with repentance and faith;
3) you are producing fruit or good deeds as evidence of your Christianity.

If after working through this book you are convinced that you are not a Christian, either because you have never understood the gospel, or because you have never rightly responded to the gospel, or because you realize that there has never been any genuine fruit in your life, then make the decision to become a Christian right now!

If you sense that God is right now working in you a biblical response of genuine repentance and faith, be sure to review the components of the gospel message on pages 10 through 15; then express to God that you are now wholeheartedly repenting of your sins and placing your faith in Christ. If this is God's work in your heart and mind, then you will undoubtedly begin to see the fruit of repentance and faith from this day forward!

YOUR STORY

Writing out your testimony (the story of how you became a Christian) can be helpful in harmonizing your experience with the teachings of the Bible. Often the temptation is to reinterpret the Bible to maintain your story. Remember that your testimony is a subjective recollection of what you think happened in the establishment of your relationship with God. The Bible is clear, objective, and timeless. God would much prefer that you reinterpret your testimony to be in sync with the clear statements of Scripture. That may mean that you need to admit that you did not really become a Christian when you thought you did. It may mean that something that you considered a "rededication" was really the point when you became a Christian and began to see fruit in your life. It may mean that what you believed to be genuine fruit at some point in your life was actually artificial and short-lived.

Whatever the case, don't be afraid to reevaluate your story especially the timing of 1) when you properly understood the biblical gospel, 2) when you rightly responded to the gospel with repentance and faith, 3) when your life began to reflect the transformation that happens when a person becomes a Christian.

Use these last few pages to thoughtfully write out "your story."

Describe the point in your life when you really understood the biblical gospel.

Describe the events that surrounded your response of repentance and faith.

Describe the fruit in your life that gives evidence of your new life in Christ.

Notes: